LIGHTHOUSES OF THE NORTHEAST

AGAINST DARKNESS AND STORM

PHOTOGRAPHS BY

WAYNE BARRETT

TEXT BY

HARRY THURSTON

NIMBUS
PUBLISHING LTD

Nimbus Publishing Limited
P.O. Box 9301, Station A
Halifax, Nova Scotia
B3K 5N5
(902) 455-4286

Design: Steven Slipp, GDA, Halifax
Printed and bound in Hong Kong

Parts of this text first appeared in "The Last Lighthouse Keeper," *Canadian Geographic*, March/April 1992. Acknowledgement is gratefully made for the permission granted by Betty June Smith and Anne Gordon Wickens to reprint selections from *We Keep A Light* by Evelyn Richardson; and by Edward Bush to use a passage from *The Canadian Lighthouse*.

Cover photo: Low Point, Cape Breton Island
Frontispiece (page iv): Rocky Harbour, Newfoundland
Back cover: Long Point, Twillingate, Newfoundland

Canadian Cataloguing in Publication Data
Thurston, Harry, 1950-
Against darkness and storm
Includes bibliographical references.
ISBN 1-55109-039-2 (Bound)—1-55109-053-8 (Pbk.)
1. Lighthouses—Atlantic Coast (Canada).
I. Barrett, Wayne. II. Title.
VK1027.A8T48 1993   387.1'55   C92-098733-8

ACKNOWLEDGEMENTS

We would like to thank the Canadian Coast Guard staff for their logistical and technical support, particularly Dave Smith and Ken Hamilton of Dartmouth, Nova Scotia, Wilfred Tucker of St. John, New Brunswick, Ivan Morrison of Charlottetown, Prince Edward Island, and Ian Gall of St. John's, Newfoundland. We are also grateful to the staff of the Public Archives of Nova Scotia, the New Brunswick Museum, Mt. Allison University Library, the Department of Transport Library in Dartmouth, Parks Canada in Newfoundland, and the Prince Edward Island Public Archives for aiding our research. Our gratitude to Noel O'Dea, Darlene Marshall, Paul Lannon of Air Nova, and Allana Sobey for her assistance; to Dorothy Blythe of Nimbus for her support in completing the book, to Anne Webb, our editor, and to graphic designer, Steven Slipp. Also, thanks to the Lighthouse Lands Preservation Committee of Albert, New Brunswick; Carol Livingston and the West Point Development Corporation of Prince Edward Island; Ernest H. Rip Irwin, Lighthouse Researcher; the helicopter pilots who brought us to remote areas, and especially the lighthouse keepers who made us welcome.
H.T. and W.B.

Special thanks to my wife Anne MacKay, my son Jason, and my daughters Laura and Amy.
W.B.

DEDICATION

To the men and women who built, maintained and served our lighthouses since their beginning.
H.T. and W.B.

For Catherine, remembering July 1, 1972.
H.T.

Contents

Prologue

My romance with lighthouses began early. On many Sundays my family would pack a picnic and drive around Yarmouth Harbour, across the causeway at The Bar and on to land's end at Cape Forchu, where the Bay of Fundy opens into the Northwest Atlantic.

The blue ocean and sky seemed endless. Under the watchful eye of my parents and that of the great lighthouse that dominated the Cape, I would spend the afternoon clambering around the razor-sharp rocks, daring them to pitch me into the sea which swirled below as it spent its force against the ledges.

Four and a half centuries before, Samuel Champlain had sailed safely by the "Forked Cape." But uncounted ships have met their fate on rocks such as these. Journeys of exploration along our coasts, unlit as they were until the 19th century, were rife with danger.

Late in the afternoon, fog would draw itself over the Cape like a grey cowl. Then the lightstation's great diaphone would blast its warning, frightening me back into reality and calling me home. Sometimes we ate supper with then lightkeeper, Herbert Cunningham. On a rare occasion, he would invite the children to climb the dizzying, spiral staircase to attend to the light. As darkness descended and we drove home, the reassuring sweep of the light would briefly brighten the fog-draped landscape before us.

I have returned to Cape Forchu many times. As a young man I took my vows of marriage there—among the irises shining like blue flames in the fog. The lighthouse seemed to stand witness.

There is an almost preternatural aura associated with lighthouses; they inexplicably conjure up their own atmosphere. A quietude surrounds them. Paradoxically, this soothing "silence" depends upon a counterpoint of sounds: the sea curling below, the cries of its winged creatures circling above (often lost from view in the enfolding fog) and the harsh report of the fog horn rending the air—a sound which reverberates through the bones of the inner ear and through the internal harp of the rib cage. Spiritually, one becomes in tune, not only with nature, but with oneself.

Whatever personal significance we might attach to lighthouses, they symbolize a universal caring for our fellow human beings. They are monuments of altruism without which our culture could not have taken root along these shores.

It was both the striking visual appeal of these monuments and their associated human stories of sacrifice that gave birth to the remarkable portfolio of lighthouses that photographer Wayne Barrett presents here. It may be impossible to pinpoint where an artist's vision begins, but in Barrett's case it could have been when the Canadian Coast Guard helicopter in which he was a passenger circled the speck of red sandstone known as Bird Rock in the Gulf of St. Lawrence. This was the loneliest lightstation in the nation. In all it claimed 11 lightkeepers' lives before it was automated. How many shipwrecks it saved we will never really know, we can only be sure that the lightkeepers' lives were not lost in vain.

In pace with the century, the lightkeeping tradition is drawing to a close. Technology, in the form of electronic, computer-controlled eyes, is rapidly replacing the keeper's vigil. Many of the proud old wooden towers also face an uncertain future, as they are being abandoned and replaced by more utilitarian steel skeleton towers. Sophisticated satellite-assisted navigation devices may one day make lighthouses obsolete.

In this context, Barrett's lighthouse portraits can themselves be seen as monuments to a passing way of life. Over the last decade he has travelled from the inner reaches of the Bay of Fundy and Gulf of St. Lawrence to the iron-bound coasts of Labrador and Newfoundland and the far-flung islands in the Gulf in order to compile a record for future generations—a record which should also be seen as an appeal for the preservation of these symbols of our seafaring history.

FACING PAGE: CAPE FORCHU LIGHTTOWER IS A MODERNISTIC IMITATION OF THE 19TH CENTURY HEXAGONAL DESIGN. TRADITIONALISTS HAVE GIVEN IT THE DUBIOUS TITLE, "THE APPLE CORE."

LABRADOR

QUÉBEC

LES ILES AUX PERROQUETS

POINTE DE L'QUEST

POINTE CARLETON

ILE D'ANTICOSTI

POINTE-DES-MONTS

CAP-DES-ROSIERS

POINTE-AU-PÈRE

GRANDE ANSE

MISCOU ISLAND

BIRD ROCK

CAPE RAY

BIG SHIPPEGAN

CHANNEL–PORT AUX BASQUES

POINT ESCUMINAC

ILE D'ENTRÉE

ST. PAUL ISLAND

CAPE NORTH

NEW BRUNSWICK

CHETICAMP ISLAND

PEI

MARGAREE ISLAND

LOW POINT

SCATARIE ISLAND

KIDSTON ISLAND

CAPE TORMENTINE

HENRY ISLAND

SYDNEY BAR

LOUISBOURG

PUGWASH

GABARUS

FOURCHU

CAPE ENRAGÉ

QUACO

ISLE HAUTE

CAPE D'OR

CHERRY ISLET
LETETE PASSAGE
HEAD HARBOUR

PARTRIDGE ISLAND

NOVA SCOTIA

POINT LEPREAU

SWALLOW TAIL

SOUTHWEST HEAD

GEORGES ISLAND

MACHIAS SEAL ISLAND

GANNET ROCK

PEGGYS COVE

CHEBUCTO HEAD

MCNABS ISLAND/MAUGHER BEACH

BRIER ISLAND
BOARS HEAD

BELLIVEAUS COVE

DEVILS ISLAND

SAMBRO

LAHAVE

MOSHER ISLAND

CAPE FORCHU

SANDY POINT

SABLE ISLAND

LOWER WEST PUBNICO
WOODS HARBOUR

MCNUTTS ISLAND

SEAL ISLAND

BARRINGTON

BON PORTAGE

CAPE SABLE

BACCARO POINT

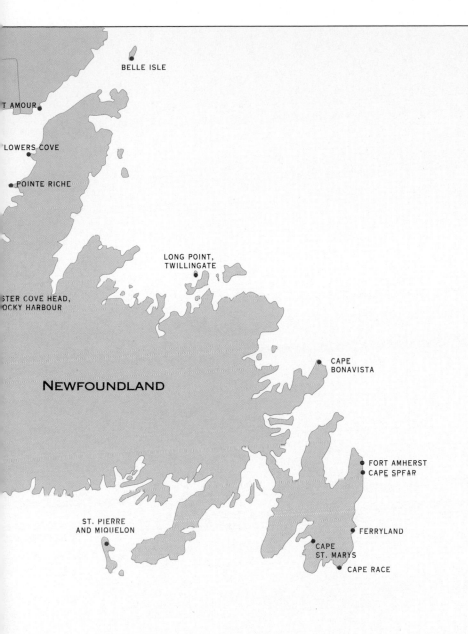

BELLE ISLE

T AMOUR

LOWERS COVE

POINTE RICHE

LONG POINT,
TWILLINGATE

STER COVE HEAD,
OCKY HARBOUR

CAPE
BONAVISTA

NEWFOUNDLAND

FORT AMHERST
CAPE SPEAR

ST. PIERRE
AND MIQUELON

FERRYLAND

CAPE
ST. MARYS

CAPE RACE

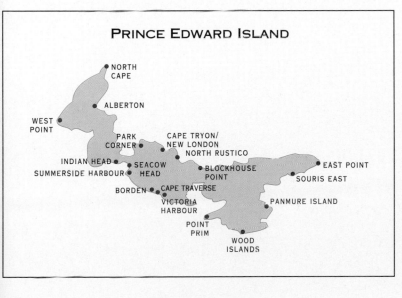

PRINCE EDWARD ISLAND

NORTH
CAPE

ALBERTON

WEST
POINT

PARK
CORNER

CAPE TRYON/
NEW LONDON
NORTH RUSTICO

INDIAN HEAD

SEACOW
HEAD

BLOCKHOUSE
POINT

EAST POINT

SUMMERSIDE HARBOUR

BORDEN

CAPE TRAVERSE

SOURIS EAST

VICTORIA
HARBOUR

PANMURE ISLAND

POINT
PRIM

WOOD
ISLANDS

INDEX OF LIGHTS MENTIONED IN TEXT

Stars in the Midst of the Ocean

ABOVE: SAMBRO LIGHTHOUSE IS THOUGHT TO BE THE OLDEST FUNCTIONAL LIGHTHOUSE ON THE CONTINENT

FACING PAGE: THE FIRST LIGHT TO SHINE FROM THE ATLANTIC SHORE WAS AT THE FRENCH FORTRESS OF LOUISBOURG. LONG SINCE DISMANTLED, A NEW LIGHT STANDS IN ITS STEAD.

When the Irish poet Thomas Moore sailed from Halifax in October, 1804, like all seaborne travellers of his day, he faced the uncertainty of a North Atlantic passage. As his departing ship hailed land's end, the reassuring glow of Sambro light inspired him to pen a poem which begins:

The murmur rose soft as I silently gazed / On the shadowy waves' playful motion / From the dim distant land, till the lighthouse fire blazed / Like a star in the midst of the ocean.

Sambro light, an 80-foot tower painted in bold red and white horizontal stripes, still stands, "like a star in the midst of the ocean," much as it did in Moore's time, warning of the granite ledges which torment the water at the entrance to Halifax Harbour. It has been standing longer than any other existing lighthouse in Canada and probably is the most venerable light on the North American continent. The thick stone walls which form the imposing hexagonal sentinel seem to have been designed to withstand volleys of canon shot, not to mention the sea's constant battering.

Today, the lightkeepers' residences are deserted. Quarterly, a helicopter sets down an electronics technician who tests the automated equipment—fog detector, fog horn, light, diesel generators. As the Canadian Coast Guard four-seater Bell helicopter circles the weathered tower, nesting terns and gulls erupt from the uncropped grass; the silhouettes of an ocean liner and a Navy frigate figure the distant horizon; the crew of a late-arriving yacht in the Marble Head to Halifax Race gaze up and wave a greeting; and a Cape Island fishing boat, with its sternsail set into the wind, bobs within the familiar and friendly range of Sambro's light and horn.

This maritime scene from the present day reaffirms the light's original purpose, outlined two and half centuries ago at the Governor's House in Halifax. On June 12th, 1752, it was resolved that "a Lighthouse at the Entrance of the Harbour of Halifax would be greatly Beneficial to the Trade, Navigation, and Fishery of this Colony, and might be the means of preserving the Lives and Properties of many of His Majesty's Subjects...." These noble objectives were met by holding a lottery and levying "Duties on Spirituous Liquors." In 1760 a sperm oil lamp cast its light from Sambro Island.

Although the history of Sambro light makes up the longest continuous chapter in the saga of Atlantic lighthouses, it was preceded by another light—the oldest in Canada—at Louisbourg. The great French Fortress on the southeastern shore of Cape Breton Island has been rebuilt in magnificent detail from its former ruins;

unfortunately, the historic lighthouse did not enjoy the same phoenix-like fate. We must reconstruct the tower from documentary evidence.

Louisbourg Harbour has hailed Spanish, Portuguese, English and French ships since the late 16th century. For many transatlantic voyagers it was the first landfall in North America. Talk of building a lighthouse only began in earnest, however, after one of the French King's ships, *Le Profond*, nearly met its end in the Harbour, then marked only by a navigational cross and an occasional bonfire.

Work began in August 1731, and the substantial 70-foot tower was completed two years later. Historical drawings indicate stone masonry construction, with four setbacks, culminating in a cupola which functioned as the lantern room. Its light might have shone in 1733, except that the 400 panes of glass shipped from France were the wrong size and could not be replaced until the following spring. On April 1, 1734, Canada's first lighthouse beam streaked across the grey North Atlantic sea and sky.

The light produced by burning cod-liver oil in a bronze basin was visible 18 miles out to sea. The by-product of this impressive beacon was a great deal of heat—and ultimately calamity. The wooden housing of the lantern caught fire on the night of September 11, 1736, gutting the lantern room. The fireproof tower survived intact.

The French quickly re-established a light, burning coal and wood on top of the stone tower. When it came time to rebuild the lantern room they resolved to make it fireproof as well. A vault-shaped brick roof, covered with lead and fitted with vents, provided a graceful covering for a bigger, safer basin which was set in a water bath in order to dissipate the heat generated by the burning oil.

The tower functioned for 20 years. Its demise was due not to any internal design flaw, but to the external forces of war. During the British siege of 1758 canon shot smashed the tower, and it was left in ruins like the rest of the town. The British built a lighthouse on the same site in 1824.

The ruins of the original light, which included several feet of exterior wall and part of an interior spiral staircase, survived into the 1920s, when they were dismantled, stone by stone, and Canada's first lighthouse passed into history.

IN his autobiography *Mirror Of The Sea*, Joseph Conrad observed: "Fogs, snowstorms, gales thick with clouds and rain—those are the enemies of good Landfalls." If so, surely lights, and lighthouses in particular, are the mariner's allies.

As long as people have been seafarers, they have required lights to guide them safely into port. The Phoenicians must have had lights. The one-eyed Cyclops in Homer's *Ulysses* may have been a symbolic lighthouse; the Greek poet Lesches mentions a lighthouse at Cape Inchisari as early as 600 BC. Priests were the first "keepers of lights," building bonfires at landfalls in Egypt. The first lighthouse that Western history records with any certainty is the great Pharos of Alexandria in Egypt.

One of the Seven Wonders of the Ancient World, the imposing white stone tower soared 512 feet from the Island of Pharos at the mouth of Alexandria Harbour. Thereafter, "pharos" became a generic term for lighthouse, and the science of lighthouse construction and illumination became known as pharology. The Pharos of Alexandria served mariners for 1600 years, until the 13th century when an earthquake brought down the venerable structure.

No lighthouse has ever equaled the grandeur of this original, but phari proliferated, following the spread of the Roman Empire across Europe. Alexander Findlay, a noted 19th century lighthouse historian, heralded them as "the marks of high civilization of those early days." Archaeologists and historians have identified the ruins of more than 30 lighthouses throughout the far-flung Roman provinces. Two of the most famous, at Dover and Boulogne, warned and welcomed early crossers of the English Channel.

The Dark Ages plunged Europe into an intellectual twilight and, at the same time, extinguished the flames of most coastal lights, although some monastic orders kept fires burning near their coastal monasteries and

hermitages. In some parishes, in Norfolk, England, for example, earthly lights blazed from church towers. Such was the tradition that lighting the coasts was considered work of Christian charity.

Ironically, the formalization of lighthouse service came about through the suppression of the monastic orders during the reign of Henry VIII. In their stead he charged The Trinity Corporation with that duty. The first statute dealing with lighthouses in the United Kingdom was enacted in 1565. It pronounced that the Corporation of the Trinity House "shall and may lawfully by virtue of this Act...erect and set up...beacons, marks and signs for the sea, in such place or places of the seashores and uplands near the sea-coasts or forelands of the sea...whereby dangers may be avoided and escaped, and ships the better come into their ports without peril."

A boon to mariners, this manifestation of social conscience was not welcomed by all coastal dwellers. In in-

CUTTING THROUGH THE FOG, THE LIGHT AT BOARS HEAD NEAR TIVERTON, NOVA SCOTIA, BEAMS ITS WARNING OF THE TREACHEROUS TIDAL CURRENTS THAT POUR THROUGH PETIT PASSAGE, BETWEEN LONG ISLAND AND THE END OF DIGBY NECK.

stances where the population depended on wrecks as a source of fuels and stores, they actually opposed the building of lighthouses. This was the case at Lizard, in Ireland, much to the dismay of the local lord, Sir John Killigrew: "The inhabitants near-by think they suffer by this erection. They affirm that I take away God's Grace from them. Their meaning is that now they shall receive no more benefit by shipwreck, for this will prevent it. They have been so long used to reap profit by the calamities of the ruin of shipping, that they claim it to be hereditary and heavily complain to me."

Notwithstanding these pockets of resistance, the number of lighthouses increased dramatically during the

golden age of discovery and colonial trade in the 16th and 17th centuries. The British lighthouse historian, D. Alan Stevenson, estimated that the number of major lighthouses world wide, excluding harbour lights, increased from 34 in 1600 to 175 in 1800. It was not until early in the 19th century that development of a system of coastal lights proceeded more swiftly in the colonies which were to become Canada. The British Trinity House oversaw lighthouse construction in New Brunswick and Nova Scotia. In Lower Canada, Québec Trinity House was created in 1805 to oversee the erection of lighthouses for the safe passage of ships on the St. Lawrence River.

MOST Old World towers were of stone masonry construction. The epitome of this style was the famous Eddystone Light, which warned of the dangers of the Eddystone Rocks, 14 miles off the port of Plymouth in southern England. The first wooden tower, 100-feet high, was

THE TWIN TOWERS OF CHURCH AND LIGHTHOUSE GRACE THE HORIZON OF GRANDE ANSE, NEW BRUNSWICK, ON THE BAIE DE CHALEUR. THEY OFFER A MESSAGE OF SAFETY FOR SOUL AND BODY. HISTORICALLY, PRIESTS WERE THE FIRST LIGHTKEEPERS AND LIGHTKEEPING WAS CONSIDERED A WORK OF CHRISTIAN CHARITY.

swept off the rocks in 1703. A second wooden tower was destroyed by fire in 1755. Its successor, completed in 1759, was a plainer monument built for durability and was a tribute to the practicality of its architect, John Smeaton. According to Alexander Findlay, it was said that "the various courses were so closely dovetailed into each other that it was almost as if the tower had been cut out of a single block." This edifice endured for more than a century.

With few notable exceptions, including the Nova Scotian Sambro and Louisbourg lights, and Point Prim on Prince Edward Island, most Atlantic lighthouses were built of lumber rather than stone. There were a number of reasons for the use of wood, including availability, cost and expediency; to build with stone would have meant unnecessary delays, and thus further loss of life.

These wooden structures proved surprisingly durable, given the harshness of a damp marine climate. The best case in point is the Gannet Rock lighthouse in the Bay of Fundy. This is a wave-swept lighthouse perching on an utterly barren rock, which the Passamaquoddy Indians called *Mekasook* or "bare place." Constructed of massive hand-hewn timbers pinned with hardwood pegs, the octagonal tower rises six stories high. Only the lighting apparatus has

been replaced since it took command of its isolated perch and the beacon was first lit on Christmas Eve, 1831. When the Coast Guard decided to demolish the aged tower in 1967, it discovered that the wood was so sound that the project was abandoned and only the light replaced.

***

THE early history of lighthouses was marked by a fierce debate over whether lights should be used to warn mariners to steer clear of dangers, or to attract them to a safe location. (Of course, today they are used for both purposes.) In Atlantic Canada the debate was focused on the most feared of places, Sable Island, the crescent of sand that swallowed ships at such an appalling rate it became known as the "Graveyard of the Atlantic."

Sir Francis Beaufort, a leading naval hydrographer of his day, argued against building a lighthouse on Sable in

his *Report on the several documents relating to the Lighthouses of the British Colonies in North America*: "Nothing however could be more mischievous than placing there a light, though more than once recommended, it could scarcely be seen further than the shoals extend and could therefore always act as an enticement to danger."

In retrospect, Beaufort's objection seems justified. Lights of the day were so feeble that they could seldom be seen soon enough to act as an early warning signal. The first lighthouses simply took the idea of a bonfire on the beach and set it atop a tower. Thus, the Cordouan lighthouse in France had an open fireplace on its summit where billets of oak were burnt; in other cases coal was used instead of wood. Coal fires were still in use in England as late as 1823. Ironically, neither material served its purpose very well at the very time it was most needed. The worst wind for mariners under sail was one blowing onshore. This same wind drove the flames of an open fire away from the view of the ships. One redeeming aspect of the open fire during fog or rain was that the fire's glow might be reflected in the atmosphere—in much the same way the sun's "fire" lingers in the sky at sunset—warning vessels of danger.

Open fires were the norm. The noble Eddystone Light was one of the first to exhibit a candelabra, which held 24 tallow candles. They often sputtered out, or alternately caused a fire.

Wicks floated in a liquid oil replaced solid candles. The British lighthouse system preferred sperm oil—the light oil collected from the braincase of the sperm whale—although a wonderful range of local variants were tried with differing degrees of success. Cod-liver oil was a common light source in Atlantic Canada. Not surprisingly, seal oil was used on Seal Island, the important landfall light at the mouth of the Bay of Fundy, and at Cape Race, Newfoundland. The latter was provisioned with 350 gallons during its first year of operation. In the Bay of Fundy, porpoise oil was preferred as it did not congeal in intense cold, as did sperm or seal oil. Supply was a problem, however, as only Indians then hunted the porpoise.

Inevitably, lighthouses changed from animal-based oils, particularly sperm oil, to vegetable oils such as colza oil refined from rape seed. Alexander Findlay outlined the reason in his 1866 classic *Lighthouses of the World*: "The untiring perseverance of the whale fishers from the neighbourhood of Nantucket has so dispersed and destroyed their prey, that it is most doubtful if a continuous and sufficient supply can be maintained, except at great prices."

In 1846, a Canadian, Dr Abraham Gesner, made a significant contribution to lighting technology with his invention of "coal oil" or kerosene. A medical doctor by training, Gesner adopted the pioneer science of geology as his avocation, and authored the first formal studies of the geology and mineralogy of his native Nova Scotia and neighbouring New Brunswick.

In Gesner's first practical experiment in the production of coal oil, he used Trinidad pitch which he obtained from a ship calling at a Nova Scotia port. The discovery of bituminous shales (called albertite) in Albert County, New Brunswick, gave him a readier source of raw material and produced a better quality illuminant.

Gesner demonstrated the suitability of kerosene for burning in home lamps in Charlottetown, Prince Edward Island. Five years later, in 1851, he was aggressively pursuing commercial applications of his discovery, including city lighting in Halifax and its use in lighthouses. Gesner claimed that it was not only cheap, but a superior source of illuminant for isolated locations, such as lighthouses, because the oil could be manufactured on site. He was granted an application to try his confidently proclaimed gas project at Maugher Beach on McNabs Island. As is the

FACING PAGE: POINT PRIM LIGHTHOUSE, THE OLDEST LIGHT TOWER ON PRINCE EDWARD ISLAND, WAS DESIGNED BY THE ISLAND'S MOST PROMINENT, 19TH CENTURY ARCHITECT, ISAAC SMITH. THE CIRCULAR BRICK TOWER RISES MAJESTICALLY TO A HEIGHT OF 60 FEET. SMITH'S ORIGINAL DESIGN CALLED FOR WOODEN CONSTRUCTION, BUT THE HOUSE OF ASSEMBLY PREFERRED A TOWER OF ISLAND BRICK. THE RUSTY RED BRICK WAS SHEATHED IN WOODEN SHINGLES IN 1847 AND PAINTED WHITE.

case with most innovators, Gesner at first met staunch resistance. Then Commissioner of Lighthouses, Jacob Miller, complained at length in a letter to the Lieutenant Governor Joseph Le Marchant of Gesner's bold scheme.

"His promised expectations fall to the ground under the serene test of practical application," Miller inveighed. "I do not by any means wish to insinuate that the gas called 'kerosene' has failed to answer any of the purposes for which it was employed as a 'light' but I would think it sufficient to state that it will never supersede 'oil light' in lighthouses, until, in the first place, the apparatus is constructed in so simple and perfect a manner, that it may be kept in perfect working order by ordinary lighthouse keepers, and not be subjected to such accidents as have attended 'the kerosene apparatus' and experiments at Maugher's Beach...."

Despite this inauspicious beginning, Gesner prevailed and his invention eventually found wide use in the Canadian lighthouse system, allowing him "to provide a long and lasting holiday for the finny monsters of the sea," those being sperm whales. Kerosene, used in flat wick lamps very similar to those common in early 20th-century homes, was only supplanted with the advent of petroleum and acetylene lamps at the turn of the century.

ABOVE: GANNET ROCK IN THE BAY OF FUNDY IS ATLANTIC CANADA'S ONLY WAVE-SWEPT LIGHTHOUSE. CAPTAIN WILLIAM OWENS REPORTED THAT ON FEBRUARY 18TH, 1842, "WAVES WASHED THE BASE OF THE LIGHTHOUSE FROM TWO TO FIVE FEET IN HEIGHT, WHICH NATURALLY CREATED GREAT ANXIETY LEST ANY BREACH SHOULD HAVE BEEN MADE IN THE FOUNDATION, WHICH WOULD HAVE EXPOSED THE WHOLE FABRIC TO BE UNDERMINED AND WASHED OFF. THE DWELLING HOUSE ATTACHED TO THE LIGHTHOUSE IS A PROJECTION OF 20 FEET TO ITS SOUTH. ALL OF THE INMATES WERE DRIVEN THENCE FOR REFUGE INTO THE BODY OF THE LIGHTHOUSE. FORTUNATELY THE TIDES WERE NEAP." SUBSEQUENTLY, A BREAKWATER WAS BUILT AROUND THE BASE OF THE LIGHTSTATION.

BELOW: THROUGHOUT THE 18TH AND 19TH CENTURIES, SPERM OIL EXTRACTED FROM THE BRAINCASE OF THE SPERM WHALE WAS THE PREFERRED ILLUMINANT IN LIGHTHOUSES. IT WAS A NOVA SCOTIAN, DR ABRAHAM GESNER, WHO INVENTED KEROSENE AND THUS GAVE "THE FINNY MONSTERS OF THE SEA" A HOLIDAY FROM RELENTLESS HUNTING. TODAY, THIS LIGHTSTATION ON LES PERROQUETS, QUÉBEC, IS USED AS AN OBSERVATION POST FOR WHALE WATCHERS INTERESTED IN PROTECTING THE WHALES WHICH AGGREGATE IN THE AREA OF THE MINGAN ISLANDS, SITE OF CANADA'S NEWEST NATIONAL PARK.

IN 1780 the Swiss born inventor Aimé Argand made the first technological advance in pharology. His search for a better lamp, which did not involve building an open fire, like many scientific "eurekas," was the product of patience, planning, and plain good luck. In this case, the inventor had to credit the inadvertent inspiration of his younger brother. His brother's account confirms the role serendipity played: "My brother had long been trying to bring his lamp to bear. A broken-off neck of a flask was lying on the chimney piece; I happened to reach over the table, and to place it over the circular flame of the lamp. Immediately it rose with brilliancy. My brother started from his seat in ecstasy, rushed upon me with a transport of joy and embraced me with rapture."

SHEEP GRAZE BESIDE THE FOG SHROUDED LIGHT AT CAPE ST. MARY'S, NEWFOUNDLAND. TAILS OF SHEEP WERE ONCE USED AS A SOURCE OF OIL FOR THE LIGHTHOUSE AT THE CAPE OF GOOD HOPE, IN SOUTH AFRICA, AND REPORTEDLY PRODUCED A BRIGHTER FLAME THAN ANY OTHER ILLUMINANT.

was critical to have some means of projecting the beams in the desired direction—out to sea. If this was not achieved, much of the light would be diffused and, for practical purposes, lost. Essentially, there are two means available for capturing and concentrating light beams: rays can be reflected by means of mirrors—the catoptric principle, from the Greek *katoptron* or mirror; or they can be deflected by making them pass through lenses—the dioptric system from the Greek *diaptrokos*, meaning to see through.

The Swedes experimented with parabolic reflectors in the 1730s with unsatisfactory results. Crude parabolic reflectors were introduced on England's Mersey River in 1763. The English trial had its origin in "a convivial meeting" among a group of scientific men in Liverpool where one of the "boys" wagered that he would read a newspaper at a distance of 200 feet by the light of a penny candle. He made good on his bet by lining a wooden bowl with putty, then embedding shards of looking glass to form a reflector. One of those present was William Hutchison, the dockmaster in Liverpool.

The American inventor Sir Benjamin Thompson elaborated on the basic design of the Argand lamp—a circular wick enclosed in a glass chimney—to include several wicks. Then, in 1827, coal gas came into use in Scotland. Thompson's apparatus was similar to a primus stove whereby the blue flame vaporized the oil under pressure and illuminated the mantle to a state of white incandescence. (Modern-day campers will recognize this system as being similar to their campfire lantern.) By the turn of the century, incandescent lights began to replace oil and gas light sources.

Not only was it necessary to produce a bright light, it

Hutchison seized upon the practical potential of the idea and installed bowl shaped mirrors, varying in diameter from three to twelve feet, behind the Mersey light. Thereafter, the catoptric system was known as the English system. Ironically, the system was perfected by J.A. Bordier-Marcet of France. His so-called "star-

lantern" used two circular reflecting metal plates, one above and one below the flame, to reflect the light horizontally to the horizon. It magnified the power of an Argand lamp seven-fold.

The use of mirrors was a dramatic improvement, but the apparatus sometimes proved cumbersome. On Machias Seal Island, reflectors, lamps and an oil reservoir almost filled the lantern room. There was so little room to manoeuver that the keepers found it difficult to carry out routine duties such as feeding and cleaning the lamps. A report, dated 1846, complained "the glass of the outer frame is so near the lamps as to be constantly misted."

The second, and most significant, breakthrough in lighthouse optics was the introduction of lenses. A French lighthouse commissioner, M. Gustin Fresnel, constructed the first lighthouse lenses by surrounding a single powerful flame in concentric rings of glass which bent the beams in the desired direction. The system became commonly known as the French system, to distinguish it from the reflector-based English system. Eventually refinements combined both the reflective and refractive principles.

Great Britain and the United States undertook conversion to the dioptric systems almost immediately. Despite the clear superiority of lenses over reflectors, the catoptric system held sway in Canada late into the 19th century, largely for economic reasons.

HEAD HARBOUR LIGHT ON CAMPOBELLO ISLAND (OR EAST QUODDY LIGHT AS IT IS KNOWN LOCALLY) DISPLAYS ITS DISTINCTIVE DAYMARK, WHICH RESEMBLES THE CROSS OF ST. GEORGE. IN THEIR REPORT OF 1842, THE COMMISSIONERS OF LIGHTHOUSES WROTE: "TO DISTINGUISH THIS LIGHTHOUSE FROM OTHERS ON THIS LINE OF COAST, A LARGE RED CROSS HAS BEEN PAINTED ON ITS EXTERIOR SURFACE WHICH CAN BE SEEN SOME MILES DISTANT WHEN APPROACHING THE PASSAGE, AND WILL BE A USEFUL GUIDE TO THOSE NOT FAMILIAR WITH THE NAVIGATION OF THIS PART OF THE BAY OF FUNDY."

IMPROVEMENTS in optic technology—better illuminants, more efficient lamps, and powerful magnifying systems—made lights more visible. For the mariner, however, there remained the problem of distinguishing between lights, especially those close to each other. Mistaking one light for another could, and often did, prove fatal.

To distinguish lights during daylight hours, they were painted with distinctive "daymarks." Coloured stripes and bands helped to differentiate between lighthouses, and made the lighthouse stand out from the surrounding landscape. In *Lighthouses of the World*, Findlay expounded on the importance of the colour of lighthouses: "When it shows against the land, white, of course, is best; and if against the sky, a dark colour is preferable. Red is sometimes used...and the extension of coloured stripes and bands is recommended. This has been particularly service-

Comrades Against Darkness and Storm

It was one of the best storms I've seen. We had a really good blow, so it was a good farewell to St. Paul," recalled head lightkeeper Paul Cranford of his last tour of duty in November, 1991, on St. Paul Island—a jagged upthrust of rock 25 kilometers off the tip of Cape Breton Island. The storm revived memories of his 16 years on this lonely Atlantic outpost; of the lightkeepers who, like himself, called St. Paul home; and of chance visitors to this wild place—storm petrels, eagles, snowy owls, and harp seals which would bark from the ice floes that hem in the Island for three months every winter. He remembered with a shudder his first summer on the Island when he tried to circumnavigate St. Paul in a sea kayak and was nearly swept away by the strong currents coiling around the rocks that have been the undoing of so many unfortunate ships.

Until its automation on November 6th, 1991, St. Paul Island was one of the few lightstations along Canada's Atlantic coast that still had resident lighthouse keepers. Knowing the tide of automation was unstoppable, in 1990 I resolved

ABOVE: THE LAST LIGHTHOUSE KEEPER ON ST. PAUL ISLAND, PAUL CRANFORD, COMPOSED LAMENTS FOR FIDDLE—"MEMORIES OF ST. PAUL ISLAND" AND "GRAVEYARD OF THE GULF"—BEFORE BIDDING FAREWELL TO THE ROCKY OUTCROP WHICH HAS LONG BEEN ONE OF THE WORST NAVIGATIONAL HAZARDS IN OUR ATLANTIC WATERS. THE LIGHTHOUSE IS NOW MONITORED BY THE CANADIAN COAST GUARD'S SLEEPLESS INTRAC COMPUTER.

FACING PAGE: THE LIGHT AT LOW POINT, NEAR NEW WATERFORD, SHINES THROUGH A FALL STORM LASHING CAPE BRETON'S ROCKY COAST. UNTIL VERY RECENTLY, LIGHTKEEPERS LAUNCHED SMALL BOATS INTO SUCH TURBULENT SEAS IN ORDER TO SAVE LIVES AND PROPERTY.

to visit St. Paul while it still had its keepers. Reaching this wind-blown Island, far from the mainland, proved daunting, however. It took six months of waiting and then, on the verge of reaching my destination, the weather again threatened to repel me. My first attempt to reach this Atlantic outpost was blown away by an icy March nor'easter. In July my seat was taken by a member of the Coast Guard maintenance crew, making a routine quarterly inspection of the lightstation's electronics. Then, in October 1990, a tempest grounded the helicopters. As I stood by, the winds blew the wind sock at a menacingly horizontal angle. "I hope you got a strong stomach," remarked Canadian Coast Guard helicopter pilot Arnie Lewis, as he greeted me in Sydney Airport. "The winds up there are pretty high."

Lewis usually depends on weather reports from Environment Canada, which receives its information on visibility and wind direction and speed continuously from an automated weather station on St. Paul Island. That day, however, the computer was out of order, so Lewis had to ask the Coast Guard Radio

in Sydney to get a direct on-the-spot radio report from the keepers on St. Paul.

Weather permitting, the pilot must make two trips to St. Paul, the first to deliver supplies and, on that occassion, myself, and the second to transport two relief keepers. Lewis confirmed that we were going to give it a try, despite a 40-knot gale. The wind buffeted our four-seater helicopter as we veered over the water while breakers angrily scratched the black slate below. Squalls drove sheets of rain which beaded on the cockpit bubble, further obscuring the mist-shrouded Cape Breton Highlands. Off Cape North, I looked down to see a Great Lakes freighter battling heavy seas, inbound for Sydney. Then, St. Paul itself loomed, its high back seemingly hunched against the storm's lashings.

Lights at both ends alert mariners to the frequently fog-bound, five-kilometer long Island. We passed over the fiberglass tower of the Southwest Point lightstation, automated in the early 1960s and now served by a solar-pow-

ered flashing light. The helicopter dipped behind the cliffs of the eastern shore, which peak at 200 meters above the swirling sea. Around a headland appeared the islet at Northeast Point, with its cluster of white, red-roofed houses and outbuildings connected by wooden walkways that thread their way through rocky outcroppings. On another day it might appear a spartan, even barren setting, but that day, it was a welcome sight.

The helicopter touched down gently on the wooden landing pad. A flurry of activity ensued as bags and goods were unloaded and others stowed aboard. I ducked my head under the blades and braced myself against the cutting wind. It was only after the helicopter lifted off to

retrieve the relief keepers from Neils Harbour, 50 kilometers south on Cape Breton Island, that I met Paul Cranford. "Typical tropical day on St. Paul," cracked Cranford, whose lanky blond hair was battened down by a toque. "Today was a touch and go day. As a matter of fact, I didn't think the chopper was coming."

There was only time for a brief tour of the Island station and its light before the helicopter would return with the relief keepers. The wind, gusting ever higher, nearly tore the red door from its hinges as we entered the light-

house and climbed the flights of steel stairs to the top of the 14-meter white concrete tower. The beacon stands on a rise 40 meters above sea level, making its light visible 28 kilometers out to sea. A more powerful light-and-lens system was replaced five years ago by a revolving light capable of being converted to solar power.

The sea was in an angry mood: two-storey waves frothed at the Island's footings of needle-sharp rocks and sent spray and foam scudding halfway up the Island's spruce-clad flanks. "Just imagine your boat coming ashore on those rocks," Cranford mused, as we stood in the lamp room. "You wouldn't have a chance, and if somehow you did make it ashore you'd find little to sustain you."

LIGHTKEEPING and lifesaving have often gone together, even though officially there were only three lifesaving stations in the Maritimes: Sable Island, Seal Island and St. Paul. John Campbell, a native of Argyllshire, Scotland,

established a lifesaving station on St. Paul Island in 1840, the same year the two lighthouses were built on the Island. Much of Campbell's duty was cause for tedium: "Upwards of seven months without any communication with any part of the world!" he lamented. "Revolutions and great changes may occur, without hearing anything about it until it be over."

Crises punctuated the long periods of inactivity, however, as on the night of May 30th, 1856: "Remarkably dense fog all day—firing the gun constantly at intervals of four hours. Fired an extra round at ten o'clock at night. About ten minutes after the gun went off we heard the ringing of a bell. A ship was on the rocks."

Campbell managed to get his lifeboat launched, despite his belief that "no boat could live in such a sea." By morning he had plucked, "with great difficulty," 70 survivors from the wreckage. Seventy-two of the Irish passengers perished, however.

Although lifesaving is no longer listed among their duties, lightkeepers have continued, until very recently, to play an active role in averting disaster at sea. Several years ago, Ingram Wolfe of Mosher Island rescued a young couple whose seven-meter sloop capsized a kilometer offshore, then proceeded to salvage the sailboat, hauling it ashore with the lightstation's tractor.

Sometimes, in a tragic turn of events, it was the lightkeepers themselves who met with disaster. The first keeper of the Northeast Light on St. Paul, Donald Moon, went in search of his two sons who had ventured onto the sea ice in February, after a seal. At dusk, a northeastern gale blew up; Moon, his two sons, and their housekeeper, who had joined him in the search, were never heard from again. It was eight days before John Campbell arrived to relieve Mrs Moon and her infant.

EVEN day-to-day lightkeeping duties could be harrowing. The lightkeeper's calling required a dedication to others that went beyond a concern for personal comfort or safety. In her article in *The Nova Scotia Historical Review*, "There's No Life Like It: Reminiscences of Lightkeeping on Sambro Island," Barbara Shaw has noted: "Before automation...few occupations carried the same responsibility for human life or demanded as much self-reliance in a continual battle with the elements, as that of the lightkeepers."

Former Sambro lightkeeper Roy Gilkie recalled that greasing the weather vane on Sambro Island was "like floating in the middle of the sky." He had to climb a ladder to the lamp room roof, then scramble onto another ladder that hugged the curved shape of the roof, in order to reach the ball. At this point, he was 115 feet above the base of the lighthouse.

In winter, especially during westerly storms, the glass would become covered with sticky snow, or ice. The keeper would have to pitch a ladder on the "tame" side of the light—the side where the winds were less gusty—and, grabbing the handles placed at intervals around the lantern, "climb around like a spider." With his free hand, Gilkie knocked the snow and ice from the glass, all the while balancing on the catwalk on the balls of his feet.

During foggy weather, before the advent of the fog horn, lightkeepers were compelled to fire warning signals at precise intervals—every ten minutes in the case of Sambro. They used a French naval deck gun. Roy Gilkie and his father Alfred once kept up this warning barrage for 368 hours, or 15 days, without missing a shot.

Before the days of electrification, the lightkeeper's duties were unrelenting, and authorities would not tolerate any lapse of responsibility in keeping the lights shining from dusk to sunrise. The keeper had to keep the clockwork mechanism that rotated the light wound through the night, "winding the clock" every three to four hours. This meant many trips up the narrow lighthouse stairs. Herbert Cunningham, who watched the Cape Forchu Light from 1922 to 1952, estimates he made 47 000 trips to the top. If it was cold and the clockwork mechanism ground to a halt, he had to manually rotate the light with a stick throughout the night.

In the morning the lenses, prisms and reflectors had to be cleaned and polished, and every summer the buildings and ironwork were painted to counter the corrosive effects of sea-spray. This constant human attentiveness to every detail of the appearance and operation of lightstations accounts for their being uncommonly pristine: they literally seem to shine in their inward and outward aspect from this constant care. It is this human touch that will be greatly missed when the last lightkeeper goes, as will the mere fact of human presence, which is reassuring to all mariners.

THE LIGHT LITERALLY SEEMS TO SHINE FROM THE HEART OF KEEPER JOE MACDONALD AT BORDEN, PRINCE EDWARD ISLAND; THIS MUST HAVE BEEN TRUE FOR THE MANY MARINERS WHO DEPENDED UPON THE LIGHTKEEPER'S EVER VIGILANT PRESENCE.

house home as assistant keeper.

During the next 30 years he saw most of the changes that automation brought with it, including the obsolescence of lightkeeping itself. Today the 400-watt mercury vapour lamp (which lasts up to five years) is rotated by a small electric motor; the fog alarm is automatically activated by a video-graph machine that takes continuous visibility readings. Frank recalls that when he took over lightkeeping duties the light was still rotated by a clockwork mechanism which he or his assistant had to wind every three hours and fifteen minutes throughout the night.

Lighting up was the day's most important task. The light source was a kerosene vapour lamp whose beam

LIGHTKEEPING was often a family affair and there are many instances of lengthy family tenures. The Gilkies of Sambro light kept the station for more than a century; the Campbells of St. Paul Island provided 72 years of service. The Cantwells of Cape Spear, Newfoundland, perhaps hold all records. Jerry Cantwell, the current keeper, is the seventh generation of his family to assume the post.

In 1991, Frank McIntosh, Prince Edward Island's last lightkeeper, ended a family tradition that saw three generations of his family watch over the 111-year-old Souris East lighthouse, the last of 76 on the Island to lose its lightkeeper. His grandfather kept the light from 1917 to 1939, until his health failed; Frank's father watched the light for three years until the war called him overseas in 1941. Frank himself was born in the cottage (a kitchen with sleeping quarters above it) that once was attached to the lighthouse. In 1960, at age 24, Frank returned to his light-

was focused through a prism made in Belgium. At Souris, Frank climbed three sets of stairs to the top of the 60-foot tower to light the lamp each evening at sunset. He first trimmed the wick, cleaned off any accumulation of carbon, and then pumped up the kerosene from the second floor. The burner was pre-heated by burning "spirits," so that when the pressurized kerosene reached it, it immediately vaporized, igniting the mantle. It was a fussy business that required a deft touch.

Once the evening lighting up was accomplished, the keeper often slept in the lighthouse. At Souris, the keepers also had to attend the breakwater light and fog alarm which were inconveniently located a half mile from the light at the end of the breakwater. In stormy conditions the breakwater might be slick with ice or washed by waves: either way it made for a perilous journey. McIntosh would try to time his run to the rhythm of the waves rolling in. Sometimes he and his assistant would rope themselves together to keep the other from going over the side.

Frank's grandfather once rowed into the storm tossed harbour, with only a storm lantern to light his way, to rescue a father and two sons whose small boat had capsized. Unfortunately a third boy was never found. On retiring, Frank was proud of the fact that there had never been a fatality at sea within range of his light. He could say without fear of contradiction: "The fishermen here have appreciated my efforts."

THE FISHING FLEET LIES SAFELY UNDER THE WATCHFUL PRESENCE OF THE SOURIS EAST LIGHT, THE LAST WATCHED LIGHT ON PRINCE EDWARD ISLAND. WHEN KEEPER FRANK MCINTOCH RETIRED AFTER 30 YEARS, HE WAS PROUD OF THE FACT THAT NO FATALITY AT SEA HAD EVER OCCURRED WITHIN RANGE OF HIS LIGHT.

LIGHTKEEPERS were inveterate record keepers, particularly of weather and shipping. None was more prodigious than Walter Butler McLaughlin of Grand Manan, New Brunswick. Part-time philosopher and poet, and full-time keeper of lights and ledgers, he became assistant lightkeeper at Gannet Rock at the tender age of 16, and at 24, in 1853, succeeded his brother as head keeper. When the Southwest Light was established in 1880 he became its first keeper, and continued in that position until 1900. Throughout this whole time, he kept a meticulous and literate journal, which in typescript runs to nearly 900 pages.

Perusing McLaughlin's voluminous records, I noted that every entry begins, "At midnight," fixing the time. This is followed by his observations on the direction and force of the wind—of keen interest to anyone concerned with the welfare of mariners in the days of sail. For

ABOVE: The keeper at Cape Race, Newfoundland, takes a romp with his four-legged friends. Lightkeepers—the mariner's best friend—were not always men, and many wives of keepers regularly shared lightkeeping duties. In some cases, women were fully responsible for a light.

FACING PAGE: High atop the basaltic cliffs of Grand Manan perches the Southwest Light. This was the scene of a daring rescue on the stormy night of February 26, 1963, when the small boat of brothers Billy and Floyd Jones was driven ashore on an icy gale. Billy climbed to the lighthouse where the keeper raised the alarm. Game warden Vernon Bagley volunteered to be lowered on a rope over the 200-foot cliffs. Bagley raised Floyd Jones of Haycock Harbour, Maine, to safety and subsequently was awarded the Carnegie Silver Medal for heroism.

example, on Christmas Day, 1897: "At midnight wind N.W. fresh breeze and cold cloudy weather, 8 degrees above zero." He noted with patriarchal pride: "We had a turkey dinner and 16 of us sat down...9 of these were my own grandchildren."

McLaughlin's last entry, dated January 1, 1900, is particularly poignant, marking as it does the passage of a personal and historical milestone. "At midnight...wind W. Strong breeze and soft thick weather with misty rain. The new century seems to shed tears at the death of the old defeated 19th century. Perhaps it would do well for all mankind to do the same...." McLaughlin, here the poet as well as log keeper, sees in the the weather his own mood, and that of humankind. "My son, J.B. Ottawa McLaughlin watched the old year and old century out and the new year and new century in. When the clock struck 12, I ceased to be a Lightkeeper and retire on an allowance of $350.00 per year after a continual service of 55 years and nine months. With much pleasure I turn the Light Station over to my son-in-law and my dear daughter his wife, whom I pray the Good God to continue to bless and keep from harm and wrongdoing."

LIGHTKEEPING has not been an exclusively male province. Officially men filled almost all lightkeeper's posts, but, in the days when families lived at the lightstations (until the late 1980s), women regularly filled in for their husbands. This fact of life is casually, but demonstratively, stated in the title of the most famous record of lightkeeping. Evelyn Richardson, in her *We Keep A Light*, clearly and quite rightly placed the emphasis on the plural, "we."

This tradition was acknowledged almost from the beginning of Atlantic lightkeeping. In the 1840s, Captain W.F.W. Owens, surveyor of the Bay of Fundy and erstwhile hermit of Campobello, commended women's involvement in lightkeeping and felt that they should be paid for their services. This must have seemed a radical idea to Victorian officialdom. After a visit to Machias Seal Island he wrote to the Commissioners of Lighthouses stating the lightkeeper's wife "ably and efficiently" assisted her husband, "besides the necessary care of her numerous family." He went on to recommend that "the present lightkeeper's

wife be paid as a reward for past services, for three or four years, £ 10 for each year with our thanks."

In a report submitted to the Commissioners in 1847, Owens recommends: "Keepers of lighthouses should all be married men, and the wives be instructed in the duties as well as the husbands for the whole work within the buildings is capable of being performed by women."

In the latter years before automation, women assumed full duties as lightkeepers. In the 1950s women watched over two of Nova Scotia's most important shipping lanes, at Scatarie Island off Cape Breton and at LaHave on Nova Scotia's South Shore. Eliza Campbell kept the light on isolated Scatarie Island for 21 years, taking over duties from her husband when he drowned off the Island. As the school was four miles from the light, she also assumed

ABOVE: SHAPED LIKE A PAWN, THE BIRD ROCK LIGHT TOWER SITS ON THE LOFTY TABLETOP OF ITS ISLAND. NOW AUTOMATED AND SERVICED QUARTERLY BY HELICOPTER, THE FLAG AND GANNETS DECLARE DOMINION OVER THIS SEAGIRT WORLD.

ABOVE RIGHT: BIRD ROCK LIGHTKEEPERS EXCHANGE WELCOME NEWS FROM THE OUTSIDE WORLD. IN APRIL 1930, THE ASSISTANT LIGHTKEEPER COMPLAINED THAT THE HEAD LIGHTKEEPER HAD FAILED TO PROCURE THE SUPPLIES THAT HE HAD REQUESTED AND, SUBSEQUENTLY, "ABANDONED US HERE ON THIS SMALL ISLAND, JUST FIVE PEOPLE AND A CHILD. THE CONDITION OF THE LATTER BROUGHT TEARS TO ONE'S EYES DUE TO LACK OF MEDICINE, AN ESSENTIAL ITEM, THE LACK OF WHICH CAUSED US ALL TO SUFFER.... HE DID NOT EVEN SEND US THE NECESSARIES OF LIFE WHICH WE REQUIRED AND WERE HERE ON THE ISLAND WITHOUT ANY KIND OF TOBACCO AND FROM THE FIRST DAYS OF MARCH WE HAD BEEN SMOKING TEA."

responsibility for the education of her three children. When she retired in 1963, she left the Island reluctantly, even though the surrounding waters had taken her husband and a son.

THE quiet life is a virtue that mainlanders often attach to lightkeeping. But with the romance of remoteness come the rigors of isolation and self-sufficiency. Bird Rock, a six-acre islet of the Magdalen archipelago in the Gulf of St. Lawrence, was considered the loneliest lighthouse posting in Canada and, consequently, the lightkeeper on this speck of land was the highest paid in the nation.

The light was established in 1870 to illuminate a new mail route between the St. Lawrence River and the Cabot Strait. The Department of Marine and Fisheries declared: "The construction of the lighthouse on this islet will be one of the most difficult pieces of work that has ever been undertaken by this Department." If building the light on the seagirt rock was onerous, living on the island was even more so. "Last fall, in landing my provisions, they all got wet with salt water; they were thrown in the surf owing to the rough time that we landed, and in the night, and were nearly lost," wrote the lightkeeper Peter Whalen in 1878.

In a letter written in 1897, the Marine and Fisheries agent in charge of the Bird Rock light outlined the litany of disasters that befell a succession of keepers: "Since it has become a lighthouse station, Bird Rock has had a very bad

LEFT: THE LOWER WEST PUBNICO LIGHTHOUSE SEEMS TRANQUIL IN ITS SETTING OF BECALMED BLUE WATERS. BUT THE LITTLE LIGHT THAT GUARDS THE FISHER'S HAVEN OF PUBNICO WAS SWAMPED IN 1954 WHEN HURRICANE EDNA SWEPT NOVA SCOTIA'S SHORES. THE STORM-TOSSED SEAS CRESTED THE CAUSEWAY, SUBMERGING IT TO A DEPTH OF SIX FEET, THEN POURED INTO THE LIGHTHOUSE ITSELF, FORCING THE KEEPER AND HIS FAMILY TO FLEE. FORTUNATELY, THEY REACHED SHORE SAFELY, NEVER TO RETURN TO THE LIGHT. LIKE ALL OTHER LIGHTS ALONG NOVA SCOTIA'S LONG COASTLINE, THIS ONE IS NOW AUTOMATED.

FACING PAGE: THE IRON TOWERS SUCH AS THIS ONE AT FERRYLAND WERE THE PREFERRED BUILDING MATERIAL IN NEWFOUNDLAND WHERE THEY PROVED VERY DURABLE. WHEN THEY DOUBLED AS HOMES FOR KEEPERS, HOWEVER, THEY MADE LESS THAN CONGENIAL LIVING QUARTERS. CONDENSATION AND HOAR FROST OFTEN FORMED ON THE WALLS, MAKING THE BUILDING OF SEPARATE RESIDENCES NECESSARY.

record. The first keeper went out of his mind and, with his assistant, was removed in consequence. The second keeper, with his son and assistant, left the island to hunt seals on the ice, and the wind sprung up; they were carried away and were never heard from again, excepting the assistant, who managed to reach [Cape Breton's] shore nearly frozen to death. The third keeper and his son were killed by the explosion of a keg of gunpowder near the fog canon. The fourth keeper was nearly killed by a premature discharge of the fog gun. His nephew and two other men died from exposure while seal hunting last winter." Although a fog alarm replaced the fatal fog canon in 1907, the tragic toll did not end. Keeper Wilfred Bourque was found dead at the foot of the 30-meter Bird Rock cliffs in March 1911. He may have fallen over after suffering a heart attack. In all, Bird Rock has claimed 11 lives, apart from shipwreck victims.

Despite the obvious danger to life and limb associated with Bird Rock, keepers there received the minimum of moral and material support from the Department. Take the case of the lightkeeping Bourque family. They had suffered repeated illness which was attributed to the rainwater. In 1897, Pierre Bourque offered to drill an artesian well free of charge, "if I do not succeed in getting water." He asked to be paid $50 if he did find water. The reply

was curt and suspicous: "The Department cannot make the arrangement suggested by Mr Bourque, but will furnish the boring tools and if water is found, as a permanent supply of potable water, will consider itemized bills for labour.up to a total of but not exceeding $50 and will pay the same when satisfied that the labour charged for has actually been performed."

Two years later, Bourque requested a supply of medicine to replace what he had used in attending to fishing folk who had come ashore—crippled, frost-bitten and starving—after three days adrift on the ice where they had survived by drinking the blood of two seals they had shot. Bourque nursed them back to health, feeding them and giving them what medicine he had in store. When he applied to restock his medicine chest, the Department refused, saying their policy was to supply only enough medicine for emergency use, such as the treatment of shipwreck victims. If Mr Bourque had dipped into his domestic supply that was too bad, he was reponsible for replacing it.

Bourque's successor, Elphage Bourque, met with a similar hard-nosed attitude when, in 1919, he pleaded with

article published in *The Nova Scotian*, she recalled the happy preparations for visitors to the isolated light: "A boatload of people never seemed to be too many. Once, as we said goodbye to one group which had been with us a week, another arrived.

"Mother made herself busy in the kitchen preparing a meal for the new arrivals. She sent one of the older children to wash the napkins and iron them dry with the flat iron which had to be heated on the wood stove. The younger children were sent to the fields to pick berries for the supper."

Although always ready with hospitality, lightkeepers and their families often had to endure less than congenial living conditions. Will R. Bird recounted the daunting state of Margaree light as reported by the Superintendant of Lights in 1857: "...the foundation of the tower was being eroded, the roof of the tower was leaky, and the keeper's wife had her kitchen in the cellar which often was flooded a foot in depth. The dampness caused by the flooding and the leaky roof caused the plaster to fall."

WOODS HARBOUR LIGHT IN NOVA SCOTIA BLINKS ITS FRIENDLY SMILE ACROSS A SEQUINED SEA.

LIGHTHOUSES are necessarily built in the most dramatic settings: pitched high on a craggy bluff, balanced on a rocky finger pointing into the sea, or rising from a remote island encircled by the seemingly endless horizon of water. There is an enforced participation in the dramatic clash of the two great natural platforms of life—land and water.

Lightkeepers came to know nature in all its aspects: not only "calm-faced Nature," as Richardson wrote, but "Nature in her tantrums, sulky and obstinate, and in her violent rages that leave one awed and helpless." Yet it is this very intimacy with the reviving force of nature, in all its moods, that the last lightkeepers seem most loathe to leave behind. Lynne Wolf, on leaving Mosher Island, said: "Sunrises are fantastic, especially before a storm. To see

the sun coming up out of the ocean is breath-taking."
Manson Murchison, the last keeper of Point Prim, the
oldest lighthouse on Prince Edward Island, reminisced:
"It's the way the moon shines on the water on a warm summer night...I miss that."

WHILE they kept watch, lightkeepers made the human
world a safer place. This fact was never stated more elo-
quently than by Evelyn Richardson, who described the
lighting up of lanterns at the southwestern end of Nova
Scotia on a stormy, wind-swept night: the lights "are the
friendly smiles of comrades in the struggle against wind
and sea, and as our lamps flash out through the murk, I
am glad they are adding their bit to the forces that fight
darkness and storm."

Technology inexorably unburdened the lightkeeper of
many responsibilities, making him or her redundant in the
process. In the Maritime region only Cape Forchu, Letete
Passage, Gannet Rock and Machias Seal Island are still attended by keepers. Only two lightstations are likely to re-
tain keepers, both in the Bay of Fundy. Lightkeepers on
Machias Seal Island lend support to Canada's claim of
sovereignty in an area of disputed marine boundaries between Canada and the United States. After bidding
farewell to St. Paul Island, Paul Cranford became the assistant head keeper on Machias Seal Island. He spent his
first Christmas there in December 1991. Fishers from

FISHERS IN THE BAY OF FUNDY WORK WITHIN SIGHT OF THE AUTO-
MATED LIGHT ON CHERRY ISLET AT THE MOUTH OF THE ST. CROIX
RIVER, NEW BRUNSWICK.

A Cordon of Lights

There are 87 major lightstations in the Maritimes and another 56 strategically scattered around Newfoundland and Labrador, in addition to nearly 1600 other navigational aids—light buoys, range lights, radio beacons, harbour lights, fog alarms, bell buoys and whistles—strung out between the head of the Bay of Fundy and the approaches to the St. Lawrence River. This constellation of lights and symphony of noise-makers outlines a safe pathway for vessels to follow along our hazardous shores.

The Atlantic Provinces are almost entirely surrounded by water. As a peninsula tenuously hinged to the rest of the continent, Nova Scotia boasts an impressive coastline of 7700 kilometers. The hinterland of New Brunswick is bracketed by 2333 kilometers of Fundy and Gulf coasts, and the St. Lawrence River reaches around its territory, providing a gateway to the heart of the continent. Prince Edward Island curves like a rusty, time-ravaged knife blade for 224 kilometers, from East Point to North Cape, with many bays, harbours and estuaries notching the red sandstone cliffs, rich farmland and white beaches in between. It is said the ironbound coast of Newfound-

ABOVE: BACCARO POINT LIGHTHOUSE IS ONE OF MANY ON NOVA SCOTIA'S SO-CALLED LIGHTHOUSE ROUTE. TO THE MARINERS OF OLD, THE GRANITE STREWN SOUTH SHORE HELD "MANY SUNKEN DANGERS."

FACING PAGE: ONE OF "A CORDON OF LIGHTHOUS-ES" GUARDING AGAINST MARINE DISASTER ON THE ATLANTIC COAST, THE RANGE LIGHT AT CAPE TORMENTINE, NEW BRUNSWICK, FLASHES ITS DISTINCTIVE RED WARNING.

land, "The Rock" that rises imperiously from the Northwest Atlantic, would circle the globe if straightened out.

It is humbling to contemplate that this entire wave-washed realm—with its uncharted islands, reefs and shoals, further confounded by tides, currents, winds and ice—lay in utter darkness two and a half centuries ago.

The Atlantic Coast was in effect a deadly trap set for explorers and settlers who set out so optimistically for the New World, in the service of empire or in search of a new start. The names of the offshore islands bear grisly testimony to the newcomers' too often shattered hopes. Sable Island, the "Graveyard of the Atlantic," has been the final resting place for more than 500 ships. Anticosti and St. Paul Island both lay claim to the dubious epithet, "Graveyard of the Gulf." The former harvested 400 ships while, on a single evening in 1835, three ships washed up on the shores of St. Paul Island, and 200 people drowned. The French-owned islands of St. Pierre and Miquelon were called "a necropolis of ships" as more than 600 are known to have foundered there in the last 200 years alone.

IN every maritime region, according to one early navigator, "many evils awaited...ships." The early commissioners of lighthouses were often at great pains to describe the hazards of their watery domains and how lighthouses, strategically placed, would do much to provide safe passage through them.

Maritime surveyor A.L. Lockwood, in his report of

1815 on a marine survey of the coast of Nova Scotia, spelled out the particular dangers of the Bay of Fundy waters: "The Bay of Fundy is considered by strangers as a dangerous navigation, and [they] approach it with caution that causes delays and frequently danger.

"The currents, fogs, gales, and ledges are blended and magnified into the terrific. I feel a thorough conviction that if the soundings of the Bay were known, and a light placed on the South Seal Island off Cape Sable, improvidence only or very particular cases would subject vessels to accident...."

Captain W.F.W. Owens, a naval surveyor, in his report of 1842, spoke from personal experience of the manifold perils of the south coast of Nova Scotia: "Perhaps no coast in the world is blest with as many and such fine Ports.... To render them available, however, for any useful or commercial purpose, it is highly necessary that the dangers, and the most distinguishable points, should be well marked by Buoys or Beacons.... This suggestion, Sirs, is not merely speculative, for Her Majesty's Ship Columbia has several times struck on sunken dangers on these coasts, which could not have occurred, had the common place precautions of proper Beacons or Buoys been used."

Nova Scotia led the way in lighthouse construction at Louisbourg in 1734 and Sambro in 1760. New Brunswick's first lighthouse was built on Partridge Island in 1791, as a beacon for ships passing in and out of fogbound St. John Harbour, the province's busiest port. Similarly, Newfoundland's first lighthouse at Fort Amherst was lit in 1813 to guide the passage of boats through the Narrows into St. John's Harbour. The first lights, as these examples show, were often built at militarily strategic points.

ÎLE D'ENTRÉE (ENTRY ISLAND), THE ONLY ENGLISH-SPEAKING ISLAND IN THE FRANCOPHONE ÎLES DE LA MADELEINE, IS SOMNOLENT IN WINTER. ISOLATED FROM THE OTHER ISLANDS BY THE SEA AND CULTURAL ANCESTRY, IT IS HOME TO THE MACLEAN FAMILY, LONG-TIME KEEPERS OF BIRD ROCK AND ENTRY ISLAND IN THE GULF OF ST. LAWRENCE.

GABARUS LIGHT, ONE OF THE BEACONS OF THE ISLAND'S "BOISTER-OUS RUGGED SHORE," IS SILHOUETTED AGAINST A STORMY CAPE BRETON SKY.

By 1834, Nova Scotia operated 11 lighthouses, five of which faced the Atlantic. At the same time, New Brunswick had five lighthouses in the Bay of Fundy—Gannet Rock, Point Lepreau, Cape Sable, Seal Island and Partridge Island. The New Brunswick commissioners were so pleased with their accomplishments in lighting their coasts, they boasted "an increase of lights would rather tend to perplex and embarrass the mariner on his voyage from the seaward."

However, there were other equally dangerous, vast bodies of water that remained plunged in darkness. In the same year as the New Brunswick commissioners were questioning whether their waters might be too well lit, shipping magnate Samuel Cunard was emphasizing the need for lights on St. Paul and the Magdalen Islands in the Gulf of St. Lawrence, and renewing calls for lights at Point Escuminac and North Cape, Prince Edward Island, at the northern entrance to the Northumberland Strait.

Cunard's fellow commissioner, J.H. Tidmarsh, gave the following bleak assessment of the unlit Cape Breton coast: "As our route from Main-a-Dieu to Louisbourg on our return lay chiefly on the seashore taking nearly the course of the beaches, it gave us a melancholy view of the numerous wrecks with which the shore is strewed, the whole coast is covered with pieces of the wreck of ships and in some coves there is an accumulation of ship-wreck nearly sufficient to rebuild smaller ones. The number of graves bore strong testimony also that some guide or land mark was wanting in the quarter to guard and direct the approach of strangers to this boisterous rugged shore."

Captain Edward Boxer pointed out a similar dire need for lighthouses on the St. Lawrence in 1828: "I found the greatest want of them, the navigation being so very dangerous, from the currents being so very strong and irregular, and the very great difficulty in getting good observations, the horizon at all times being subject to so great an elevation and depression, and there not being even one [lighthouse] in the whole Gulph. It was truly lamentable, Sir, the number of wrecks we saw on the different parts of the coast...for the number of lives lost must be very great, and property incalculable."

LIGHTHOUSES were critical to the economic development of the colonies, as Thomas Corwin observed in his 1851 *Report On The Trade and Commerce of the British North American Colonies:* "...each of the colonies is making exertion for an additional number of lights upon its coast...being fully impressed with the principle so well understood in our country that the extent to which the shores of a country are girdled with lights may be considered a fair index to which the intelligence, industry and prosperity pervade its inhabitants."

At Confederation, all the lighthouses came under the jurisdiction of the new country of Canada. The Dominion entered a period of intensive lighthouse construction. In 1872, the Minister of the Department of Marine and Fisheries—which took over responsibility for lights from Trinity House—reported that, in its first five years, his Department had built 93 lights and had another 48 under contract. In the three decades following Confederation, the number of lighthouses trebled to stand at 769 in 1900.

Most of these towers were of heavy timber construction. In 1904, Colonel William Anderson, Engineer-in-Chief at Marine and Fisheries, justified the government's decision to use home-grown materials: "By adopting cheap wooden lighthouses and placing in them illuminating apparatus not too complicated to be operated by the uninstructed lightkeeper...it was possible to rapidly surround our coasts with a cordon of lighthouses, not of first-rate quality possibly, but sufficiently effective to give valuable aid to our growing commerce."

In Newfoundland prefabricated iron towers were preferred to wood. In 1885, J.T. Nevill, the Inspector of Lighthouses, reasoned: "The use of course adopted here of using cast iron for the Light towers has been illustrated by the destruction, by fire, of the wooden structure erected by the Dominion Government at Cape Ray. Wood is usually adopted because it is somewhat cheaper than iron; but one or two losses by fire would soon more than cover the difference.... Further, iron is permanent, it may be said everlasting, and even requires less attention to painting than is required by perishable structures of wood."

Economy and expediency may have been foremost considerations in the race to light the coast, but there were titans among Atlantic lighthouses, such as the great lighthouse at Cape Race, Newfoundland. The hyper-radial light produced a flash of more than one-million candle power At the turn of the century, Cape Race was considered to be the finest lighthouse in the world, and still today it is Canada's preeminent light.

"By all odds the famous Cape Race lighthouse, commanding the busiest shipping lanes on the approaches to British North America, was the most important landfall light ever established on our shores," according to the Canadian lighthouse historian, Edward Bush. Pitched on 178-foot seaside cliffs, it is the first light mariners see upon crossing the North Atlantic.

British historian Frederick Talbot wrote in 1913: "More fearful catastrophes have been enacted within hail of the lights at Cape Race and Cape Ray...and more millions sterling of cargo and ships have been shattered and lost here than upon any other corresponding stretch of coast in the world." No doubt he wrote this indictment with the sinking of the *Titanic* fresh in his mind. In 1912, the world's most palatial, and supposedly unsinkable, ocean liner struck an iceberg and went down, taking with it 1552 crew and passengers. The *Titanic's* radio officer was transmitting passengers' personal messages to the radio relay station at Cape Race until ten minutes before the collision and, as a result, may have ignored a warning from a nearby ship, the *Californian*, about hazardous ice conditions.

FUNCTION, more than anything, determines the type and size of a lighttower and the power of the light shown from it. Lighthouses fall into four principal categories: 1) landfall lights, 2) major coastal lights, 3) secondary coastal lights, and 4) harbour lights.

Landfall lights are the advance guard. To a ship making transatlantic passage, they announce that land has been

MISCOU LIGHT GUARDS THE GILDED SHORES OF MISCOU ISLAND. "THE NUMEROUS LOSSES OF SHIPPING ON THE SHORES OF THIS ISLAND" CAUSED THE COMMISSIONERS OF LIGHTHOUSES OF THE GULF OF ST. LAWRENCE TO PRESS THE LIEUTENANT GOVERNOR OF NEW BRUNSWICK TO BUILD A LIGHT "ON THE MOST EASTERLY POINT, WHERE...A LIGHT COULD BE SEEN FROM THE HARBOURS OF GRAND AND LITTLE SHIPPEGAN, BY ALL VESSELS ENTERING AS WELL AS DEPARTING FROM HALIFAX TO QUÉBEC...."

FACING PAGE: CONSTRUCTED IN 1856, MISCOU ISLAND LIGHT IS ONE OF THE FEW WOODEN, OCTAGONAL, TAPERED TOWERS WHICH HAVE SURVIVED SINCE THE PRE-CONFEDERATION PERIOD IN CANADA.

TOP: RANGE LIGHTS AT ALBERTON, PRINCE EDWARD ISLAND, GUIDE A FISHER TO A SAFE HAVEN. RANGE LIGHTS MARK THE FINAL ENTRANCE TO A HARBOUR. ERECTED IN PAIRS, THEY ARE PLACED SOME DISTANCE APART AND AT DIFFERENT ELEVATIONS. WHEN BOTH LIGHTS ARE LINED UP ON APPROACH, THE PILOT IS ON THE CORRECT PATH TO ENTER A HARBOUR OR CHANNEL, OR TO AVOID A DANGER TO NAVIGATION.

BOTTOM LEFT: ALL TOWERS—WHATEVER SHAPE OR HEIGHT—ARE TOPPED BY A LANTERN WHICH IS USUALLY PAINTED RED LIKE THIS ONE AT MARGAREE ISLAND, CAPE BRETON. THE LANTERN HOUSES THE LIGHT ITSELF, SOMETIMES REFERRED TO AS "THE SOUL OF THE LIGHTHOUSE."

BOTTOM RIGHT: LIGHTS FROM LIGHTSHIPS SHINE NO MORE. THE LAST CANADIAN COAST GUARD LIGHTSHIP WAS THE *LURCHER,* WHICH WAS ANCHORED ON THE LURCHER SHOAL IN THE BAY OF FUNDY. LIGHTSHIPS HAVE BEEN REPLACED BY FLOATING MARINE AIDS OR BUOYS, WHICH ARE SOLAR-POWERED.

BRIER ISLAND, N.S.

In 1895, Joshua Slocum, Brier Island's most famous son, became the first man to sail alone around the world. Before setting out on his historic voyage, Slocum made a nostalgic stopover at his Island birthplace. He wrote of his return in *Sailing Alone Around the World*, a book that earned him the sobriquet, Thoreau of the Sea: "...the *Spray* sailed directly over the southwest ledge through the worst tide-race in the Bay of Fundy.... I was delighted to reach Westport. Any port at all would have been delightful after the terrible thrashing I got in the fierce sou'west rip."

One cannot help but think that Slocum's home waters somehow prepared him during his childhood for his exploits in later life. They certainly served as a healthy reminder of the treachery of the sea as he embarked on his solo circumnavigation of the planet's waters. The tide rips

that coil around Brier Island were a compelling enough reason for the erection, in 1809, of a lighthouse for the safety of all mariners.

The first lighthouse proved minimally efficient and came in for criticism from all quarters. By 1832, however, the Brier Island light had been rebuilt and the wooden lantern replaced with a metal one which gave "fair light." A new lamp was on order and when installed "that Lighthouse will be equal to any," reported Commissioner Thomas Barlow. However, he added this pessimistic note: "I know of no place at present within the Bay of Fundy that requires a further expense for Light Houses. The Fogs that prevail in our Coasts is the principal cause of ship wrecks and I think it almost impossible to remedy that evil."

The Brier Island light, although it cannot remedy the fogs, remains a reassuring beacon for mariners troubled by the turbulent waters that so impressed Slocum.

PREVIOUS PAGE: ENTRANCE TO HALIFAX HARBOUR.

CAPE FORCHU, N.S.

Samuel de Champlain called the grey points of land Cape Forchu, or "Forked Cape," when he sailed by them in 1604 on his way up the Bay of Fundy. A light first shone from the knife-shaped rocks of the Cape in 1840. It was much needed, not only because of the ominous fogs and less than ideal harbour, but because of Yarmouth's distinction in the shipping trade. In 1876, the author of the Shipping Record of the town could claim that Yarmouth "stands unrivalled among the Ports of the world in the value and tonnage of her Shipping, proportionate to its population."

An original Fresnel lens, weighing 3300 pounds and sporting 360 prisms, welcomed and bade farewell to Yarmouth's ships. Today, that lens is housed in the Yarmouth Museum, along with other memorabilia of the Golden Age of Shipping.

The old timber tower, so beloved by photographers, is also gone—a victim of the Cape's damp climate. It was re-placed by a conspicuously modern, needle-shaped concrete tower in 1962. Local residents loudly protested the demolition of the picturesque old light, and demanded that a replica be built to replace it. By way of concession, designers substituted a hexagonal design for a circular tower, but the result was of dubious aesthetic success as its nickname, "the apple core," attests.

A two-foot by six-inch mercury vapour lamp, of 2000 000 candle power projects its beam 30 miles out to sea, re-assuring the many small-boat fishing folk who ply these waters. Although Yarmouth's shipping heyday is long past, it remains one of the most important fishing ports in Atlantic Canada and the terminus for the New England passenger ferry.

The light itself is automated, but the Cape Forchu lightkeeper's residence now serves as a monitoring station for 20 automated lighthouses in western Nova Scotia between Digby and Port Medway.

KIDSTON ISLAND, N.S.

The Kidston Island light at Baddeck overlooks the inland seas of the Bras d'Or Lakes on Cape Breton Island. This sun-spangled scene was familiar to Alexander Graham Bell who summered nearby at his beloved estate, Beinn Bhreagh.

MARGAREE HARBOUR, N.S.

Range lights mark the entrance to Margaree Harbour, at the mouth of Cape Breton Island's most famous salmon river, the Margaree. Such minor lights operate only seasonally, usually from April to December, due to ice conditions in the Gulf of St. Lawrence.

NEW LONDON

Launched in St. John, New Brunswick in 1851, the *Marco Polo* was known as "the fastest ship in the world." Its return trip from England to Australia in five months, 21 days was a record that stood all challenges by other clipper ships. In July 1883, the *Marco Polo*'s illustrious career came to an end on the sand bars five miles east of the New London light on Prince Edward Island. The ship was carrying pitch pine from Montmorency, Québec to Liverpool, England when a Gulf gale drove it ashore.

One of the eyewitnesses was the young Lucy Maud Montgomery who, like the *Marco Polo*, would earn a world wide reputation. Montgomery later described the wreck of this famous vessel as the most dramatic event of her childhood.

INDIAN HEAD

Dating from Prince Edward Island's shipbuilding heydey, the light-house at Indian Head (historically known as Indian Point) has marked the entrance to Summerside Harbour since 1881. The octagonal tower rising from the centre of a concrete foundation is a now rare design once favoured where there was little or no room for a keeper's house. In fact, a lightkeeper never lived in the three-room quarters, but instead rowed out each evening and remained there until morning. A breakwater protects the foundation of the little light from waves and ice.

North Cape

The North Cape lighthouse presides over the longest rock reef (nearly one mile long) in North America. According to Islanders, it is also situated in the windiest spot on what is a notoriously wind-swept Island. These two hazards to shipping—wind and hidden rocks—combined with the fact that North Cape naturally marks the northern entrance to the Northumberland Strait, should have made North Cape one of the first places where a light was erected. However, this was not the case. Point Escuminac, on the New Brunswick shore, marked the other side of the Strait in 1841, a quarter of a century before its sister light flashed a greeting across the Strait's waters.

As early as 1834 the Beaufort Report made a concerted plea for a light at the Cape: "On the N.W. Point of Prince Edward Island, a light would be highly useful to vessels who crossing the Gulf are forced down in the bight by violent N.E. winds. The rapidly increasing trade of Miramichi and the many rising settlements in the Strait of Northumberland, would also well justify the erection of a lighthouse there."

No one seemed to argue the need for a lighthouse, but neither would anyone foot the bill. The House of Assembly's request to the governments of the British North American colonies, the United States, and even Great Britain for "proportionate contributions" based on shipping volume fell on deaf ears.

Finally, residents succeeded in embarrassing the Island's government into action. They rigged a portable lamp on a makeshift stage to mark the Cape, and the government responded on March 22, 1865, with a grant of $2000 for a proper lighthouse. It cost more than $5000 and opened in 1865.

The 63-foot high North Cape Lighthouse is a classic example of the pre-Confederation octagonal wooden towers, and one of the few still standing. When the Dominion of Canada assumed responsibility for Prince Edward Island's lighthouses in 1873, the Department of Marine and Fisheries found the light inadequate for the lighthouse's importance, and subsequently replaced the fourth order dioptric light with a catoptric light in 1875. Otherwise it remains essentially unchanged—a testament to the sturdy wood construction and skill of the 19th century carpenters.

The lightkeeper's dwelling, which is no longer present, was exposed to the full fury of the elements, as one keeper's records of 1949 attest: "The sea spray when winds are on shore, is very uncomfortable and, during cold weather, causes a heavy coating of slush and ice to form on and about the house; at times this condition has sealed up the doors of the dwelling and necessitated the lightkeeper having to chop his way out."

CAPE SPEAR

The oldest existing lighthouse in Newfoundland is pitched atop 65-meter cliffs at Cape Spear, the most easterly point of North America. The historic structure is an excellent example of the stone towers typical of early 19th century lighthouse construction in Newfoundland. A tower built from rubble supports the lantern and prism, and this central core is surrounded by a two-storey, square wooden-frame residence for the lightkeepers.

The Cape Spear lighthouse [PREVIOUS PAGES], built in 1834-35, was the first public project undertaken by the Newfoundland government after it was granted representative government in 1832. It served primarily as a directional light for St. John's Harbour. Ships approaching St. John's from the south and east were first sighted from this promontory jutting into the Atlantic.

At the behest of the St. John's Chamber of Commerce, a flag signal system was put in place at Cape Spear in 1839. Each merchant house in St. John's was equipped with its own flag. When the lightkeeper hailed a ship flying a merchant's flag, he or she raised the same banner from the crosstree of the flagstaff to relay the sighting to the signal station at Signal Hill, where it could be seen from the city. This system seems to have prevailed throughout the 19th century.

The old lighthouse functioned until 1955 when a new concrete lighttower was erected a few hundred feet away. Declared of national historic importance by the Historic Sites and Monuments Board, the interior and exterior of the original light station have been restored to reflect the 1839-40 period. Included among the artifacts are the tools of an early 19th-century lightkeeper's trade: lamp glasses, polishing rouge, chamois skins, linen rubbing cloths, trimming knife, linseed oil, flax, tow, sponges and brushes—all needed to keep the light shining brightly, from sundown to sunup.

A "substantial paling fence" was erected along the edge of the cliffs in 1858. It no doubt served to secure a playground for the lighthouse children. Today, restored in all its pallid grandeur, it protects the 70 000 visitors to the historic site from harm's way.

The new concrete light is watched by a member of the Cantwell family, as it has been since 1846. That year, the ship *Rhine* was fog bound at the mouth of St. John's Harbour. On board was Prince Henry of the Netherlands. James Cantwell, a harbour pilot at the time, rowed out and safely guided the ship with its royal cargo through The Narrows and into the Harbour. As a measure of his gratitude the Prince penned a letter of recommendation, asking that Cantwell be considered for the position of lightkeeper at Cape Spear. Cantwells have kept Cape Spear ever since. The current keeper, James Cantwell, is the ninth in his family to tend the light—the sixth generation. He may be the last as the Coast Guard's automation program has reached Newfoundland's rocky shores.

Born at the lightstation, Cantwell has commuted to his duties since the station was reduced to "bachelor status" in 1971. "When the families are removed from the station," Jerry explained, "the attitude changes. Keeping the light is no longer something the family does to survive as a family and for the service of those at sea. Other people get up in the morning and go to the office. I get up in the morning and go to Cape Spear."

Not only has the number of lightkeepers been reduced in recent years, but their importance and prestige in Newfoundland outport society has also declined. In the 19th century, a keeper's salary afforded a comfortable standard of living commensurate with middle-range civil servants. What was perhaps more important was that lightkeepers were assured of a regular salary unlike most of their neighbours who were dependent upon the vagaries of the cod fishery. Lightkeepers also formed one of the vital links to the outside world for isolated Newfoundland outports. This pride in the lightkeeping tradition has been carefully preserved in the Cape Spear restoration.

Fort Amherst (St. John's)

With wind in his sails, Sir Humphrey Gilbert slipped through the St. John's Narrows on August 3, 1583, to claim Cabot's "newfound" land for England. Basques and Portuguese are thought to have coasted and fished the shores of "The Rock" before Cabot's landing in 1497. Still, it would be more than 300 years before a light guided mariners to safety along this ironbound coast.

The first lighthouse in Newfoundland was built in 1813 at Fort Amherst, at the entrance to St. John's Harbour. Voluntary contributions from the fishing fleets that harvested the Grand Banks' finny bounty main-tained the original light until the Newfoundland colonial government was formed in 1832. In 1852, a new house, lantern and optic were erected, and they still beam a welcome to St. John's Harbour.

During the 19th century a heavy piece of ordinance—a "fog canon"—was discharged at the fort every hour when the Cape was shrouded in fog. The sound helped to guide vessels through The Narrows.

Towering high above the light is the port's famous landmark of Signal Hill, where Guglielmo Marconi received the first transatlantic wireless message on December 12, 1901, in a hospital near Cabot Tower.

LONG POINT, TWILLINGATE

"Twillingate Long Point Light Station is more than a beacon marking a point of land; it has been and still is, a life-saving station.... Many a sealer or bird-hunter has been warned of approaching foul weather or ice movements by the manually operated horn...." Such pronouncements by local mariners have made clear the need for this lightstation to be occupied by a keeper, rather than being automated.

The lightstation is not only distinguished by its service to the community, but also by its architectural features. The house, a fine example of Newfoundland-Irish vernacular architecture, reflects the town's prominence as the centre of the 19th century seal fishery in Notre Dame Bay. It is linked to the fog alarm building by a covered walkway. This rare feature, found at only two other lightstations in Newfoundland, affords the keepers a sheltered passage from their hearth to workplace. Originally the fog alarm was located as far from the residence and as close to the water's edge as possible. The fog alarm building, now home to an electronically activated fog alarm, once sheltered a diaphone. Invented by J.P. Northey of Toronto in 1902, this complex apparatus—tanks for compressed air, diesel engines, sound-producing pistons, large flywheels and fan belts—set the building pulsing with sound and motion. Such buildings are becoming increasingly rare, however, as most fog alarms are now so small that they can be mounted on the sides of lighthouses.

The lighttower itself is perhaps the station's most distinctive and visually charming feature. It appears to be unique among Canadian lighthouse designs. The tower was made of brick set in portland cement. It proved sturdy enough to survive the 1929 earthquake off the Grand Banks, although it sustained some cracking. Subsequently the whole tower was glazed with a foot-thick coating of steel-reinforced concrete.

The all red tower—its distinctive daymark—rises from a square base and then angles inward at the upper corners, above which it is divided into 24 facets. The lantern, with its triangular panes, echoes this pleasing geometric complexity. The triangular glass bars and panes that combine to support the heavy domed cap are features common in the British Isles, and reflect Newfoundland's close association with Britain prior to Confederation. Simpler, less expensive designs were generally preferred by engineers of the neophyte country of Canada.

The fog alarm building, covered walkway, light tower and residence combine at Long Point lightstation to make "a picturesque assemblage." In the spring, the lightstation is an ideal lookout for the parade of giant icebergs swept south on the Labrador Current.

The West Point lighthouse, a distinctive square tapered tower, was built in 1875. In 1912 its traditional red and white colouration was changed to black and white horizontal stripes. The light, a beloved symbol of the community of fishing folk, was automated in 1963. At the same time, the Coast Guard demolished the keeper's dwelling. Unwatched, the tower stood alone, and became the object of vandalism. "Those who grew up here felt terrible about the state of the lighthouse," recalls Carol Livingstone, the wife of a fisher and granddaughter of "Lighthouse Willie," the first West Point keeper who kept watch for half a century.

Livingstone spearheaded the formation of a community action group—the West Point Development Corporation—which made the restoration of the lightstation its priority. The group rebuilt the keeper's dwelling and converted it into a chowder kitchen, craft shop and guest rooms. In 1988 they opened the Tower Room, complete with 15-foot ceilings and three windows on the sea, which has become a popular destination for honeymooners. The light is one of only two in Canada that have been restored for tourist accommodation, the other being on Brandypot Island at the confluence of the Saguenay and St. Lawrence rivers.

Where there is no community support for the preservation of the lights, hope is dim for their future. Until

FACING PAGE: THE FOURTH BUILT IN NEWFOUNDLAND, CAPE BONAVISTA LIGHTHOUSE WAS COMPLETED IN 1843 TO SERVE THE DEVELOPING LABRADOR FISHERY AND SEALING INDUSTRY ON THE NORTHEAST COAST OF THE ISLAND. THE ORIGINAL LIGHT, A CATOPTRIC SYSTEM CONSISTING OF 16 ARGAND LAMPS AND REFLECTORS, CAME FROM THE FAMOUS BELL ROCK LIGHTHOUSE ON THE EAST COAST OF SCOTLAND. THIS WAS REPLACED BY A CATOPTRIC SYSTEM FROM THE ISLE OF MAY, SCOTLAND, IN 1895 AND SERVED UNTIL 1962. IT IS STILL ON DISPLAY IN THE LANTERN OF THE OLD LIGHT TOWER, WHICH WAS CONSTRUCTED OF CUT STONE IN ORDER TO SUPPORT THE GREAT WEIGHT OF THE LIGHTING APPARATUS. TODAY, AN ELECTRIC LIGHT SUPPORTED ON A STEEL TOWER SERVES MARINERS.

ABOVE: THE REPLICA OF THE SEAL ISLAND LIGHT, IN BARRINGTON PASSAGE, NOVA SCOTIA, IS A PROUD MONUMENT TO THE PHILAN-THROPY OF MARY CROWELL HICHENS. IN 1823 SHE AND HER HUS-BAND RICHARD HICHENS ESTABLISHED THE FIRST LIFESAVING STATION IN CANADA ON SEAL ISLAND, WHERE SHIPWRECKED SAILORS INEVITABLY PERISHED. HOWEVER, AFTER THE HICHENS MOVED TO THE ISLAND NO ONE WAS EVER AGAIN LOST ON ITS SHORES. WHEN A LIGHTSTATION WAS ESTABLISHED THERE IN 1831, RICHARD HICHENS BECAME THE FIRST LIGHTKEEPER.

recently, there has been little coordinated effort, regionally or nationally, to save Canada's lighthouses. In the United States, however, The Lighthouse Preservation Society was formed in 1987 to facilitate the transfer of ownership of accessible lighthouses to the National Park Service, state parks, towns, non-profit organizations and private individuals. Furthermore, they persuaded Congress to pass the $3 million federal Bicentennial Lighthouse Fund, a matching grants program that has assisted more than 150 local communities in restoring their lighthouses.

In Canada, current federal policy calls for the disposal of obsolete lightstations, and the so-called surplus federal lands which they occupy, to the highest bidder. The

ABOVE: RESTORED BY THE COMMUNITY, THE WEST POINT LIGHT-HOUSE AND KEEPER'S QUARTERS HAVE BECOME A POPULAR TOURIST DESTINATION AND THE BACKBONE OF THE COMMUNITY'S DEVELOPMENT. VISITORS CAN CLIMB THE 67-FOOT TOWER, FOLLOWING IN THE WELL WORN STEPS OF "LIGHTHOUSE WILLIE," KEEPER FROM 1875 TO 1925. AFTERWARD THEY CAN EAT IN THE CHOWDER KITCHEN AND STAY THE NIGHT IN THE TOWER ROOM OR KEEPER'S QUARTERS.

FACING PAGE: THIS QUAINT LIGHT WHICH ONCE SERVED CAPE TRYON, WAS MOVED TO PARK CORNER, PRINCE EDWARD ISLAND, WHERE IT IS NOW USED AS A SUMMER COTTAGE.

government is resolute in its determination to receive "fair market value" for the keepers' houses and lands, even when disposing of them to other government departments. Some feel that this "free market" philosophy prejudices citizens' efforts to save lights and lands at the centre of their history and hearts. As a result, there is grass root opposition to the government's privatization initiative.

In response to efforts to sell the lands attached to Swallow Tail light on Grand Manan Island—one of the most scenic and frequented lights in the region, and designated as a national historic site—a committee was formed to campaign for local ownership. A regional group, Lighthouse Lands Preservation Committee, also came into be-

ing to fight for the preservation of other Bay of Fundy lights and lands slated for the auction block. Members argue that, in many instances, the lights' locations are more important than the lights themselves. Often lighthouses are located on headlands which must have served aboriginal peoples as look-offs. Early navigators used the same landmarks to explore these "newfound" lands. Similarly, fishers and other mariners depended upon these prominent features even before they were lit.

Because lighthouse lands often jut into the ocean, they create their own currents and this mixing often results in high marine productivity. They are ideal locations for both the study and enjoyment of nature's spectacle. I have stood

LITTLE LIGHTS SUCH AS THIS ONE IN VICTORIA, PRINCE EDWARD ISLAND, ARE INDISPENSABLE PARTS OF THE TOWNSCAPE AND, TO SOME, THE VERY SYMBOL OF THE VILLAGE'S PROUD PAST. SINCE 1990 IT HAS HOUSED THE VICTORIA SEAPORT MUSEUM AND ANCHORED A VILLAGE WALKING TOUR.

at Swallow Tail light watching the human commerce of lobster boats, herring seiners and passenger ferries and, at the same time, witnessed the spectacle of humpback and right whales spouting and cavorting offshore with their smaller cetacean cousins, harbour porpoises.

Often lighthouse lands provide the only easy public access to the coast. Tourists often visit them to paint or photograph the old towers in their dramatic settings. Local

ABOVE: The old lighttower at Pugwash looks out of place in its rustic setting. It was replaced in 1962 by a new skeleton tower and moved to a nearby farm where it now serves as an outbuilding.

FACING PAGE: Land's end at Cape Enragé gives way to a panoramic view of the Bay of Fundy. Privatization threatens public access to lighthouse lands which many consider to be community commons.

residents frequently picnic at the lights and have come to view them as community commons. People come to these special places for the peace that they offer.

The Lighthouse Lands Preservation Committee wants to ensure that access to these sites is preserved for future generations, and that they are used in a manner that protects their ecological, historical and social integrity. In order to maintain and enhance the public interest in such sites, they are advocating that they remain public property (government owned) or be held in public trust.

Three decades ago, the Richardsons of *We Keep A Light* set a worthy precedent for the dispensing of lighthouse lands when they bequeathed their Bon Portage Island acreage to Acadia University to serve as a living laboratory and field station in their ecology program. Currently, conservation groups on Brier Island, Nova Scotia, and

Campobello Island, New Brunswick, are working to convert existing lightstation buildings and surrounding lands into marine research and education facilities.

Perhaps the greatest threat to the lighthouses themselves is posed by the advance of navigational technology. Satellite aided navigation could soon make even major coastal lights obsolete. Furthermore, the cost of maintaining these aging structures is escalating, at the same time as government funds are shrinking.

The Federal Heritage Review Buildings Office is conducting assessments of all lighthouses in the region over 40 years of age. Those deemed to have significant heritage value will become either designated or registered historic buildings. Registered status prevents any alterations to either the exterior or interior of the buildings, whereas designated status allows for limited architectural changes. At least this exercise holds out hope that some lightstations will be preserved.

Whether or not lighthouses continue to be part of our seascape ultimately rests with us. In spite of their steady demise, they show no sign of giving up their hold on our imagination. Lighthouses remain the strongest shared symbol of our maritime culture. As such they beg our continued stewardship. Keeping the lights means keeping alive the values that have made us who we are.

PREVIOUS PAGE: THE SUN SETS IN A BLAZE OF GLORY BEHIND THE LIGHTHOUSE ON BRIER ISLAND, NOVA SCOTIA. HOW LONG THESE FAMILIAR TOWERS WILL REMAIN A PART OF THE SEASCAPE IS UNCERTAIN DUE TO THE SWEEPING AUTOMATION MOVEMENT OF THE LAST THREE DECADES, AND EVER ADVANCING NAVIGATIONAL TECHNOLOGY.

SELECTED BIBLIOGRAPHY

ALLABY, ERIC. GRAND MANAN. GRAND MANAN MUSEUM INC., 1984.

ANDRIEUX, JEAN-PIERRE. SHIPWRECK, MARINE MISADVENTURE IN STORY AND PICTURE FROM THE TREACHEROUS SHORES BEYOND. BEAMSVILLE, ONTARIO: W.F. RANNIE, 1975.

APPLETON, THOMAS E. USQUE AD MARE, A HISTORY OF THE CANADIAN COAST GUARD AND MARINE SERVICES. OTTAWA: DEPARTMENT OF TRANSPORT, 1968.

BAIRD, BETTY. "AND NOW—A LIGHTHOUSE FOR THE CAPITAL CITY," CANADIAN GEOGRAPHIC, VOL. 101, NO. 2, 1981.

BAIRD, DAVID M. "LIGHTHOUSES OF CANADA," CANADIAN GEOGRAPHIC, VOL. 102, NO. 3, 1982.

___. "LIGHTHOUSES," THE CANADIAN ENCYCLOPEDIA. EDMONTON: HURTIG PUBLISHERS, 1988.

BEAVER, PATRICK. A HISTORY OF LIGHTHOUSES. LONDON: PETER DAVIES, 1971.

BIRD, WILL R. "NOVA SCOTIA HAS MANY LIGHTS," CANADIAN GEOGRAPHICAL JOURNAL, VOL. 54, NO. 3, MARCH 1957.

BRUCE, HARRY. "SENTINELS BY THE SEA," IMPERIAL OIL REVIEW, SPRING 1991.

BRUCE, HARRY, WAYNE BARRETT AND ANNE MACKAY. THE GULF OF ST. LAWRENCE. TORONTO: OXFORD UNIVERSITY PRESS, 1984.

BUSH, EDWARD F. THE CANADIAN LIGHTHOUSE. CANADIAN HISTORIC SITES NO. 9. OTTAWA: INFORMATION CANADA, 1975.

CANADIAN COAST GUARD. ATLANTIC COAST LIST OF LIGHTS, BUOYS AND FOG SIGNALS. OTTAWA: MINISTRY OF SUPPLY AND SERVICES, 1991.

THE CITIZEN. "LIGHTHOUSE KEEPERS SHOULD BE RETAINED," 5 JULY 1986.

DE GARTHE, W.E. PEGGY'S COVE. HALIFAX: W.E. DE GARTHE, 1956.

DUFFY, PETER. "GRAVEYARD OF THE GULF," THE NOVA SCOTIAN, 13 NOVEMBER 1982.

FINDLAY, ALEXANDER. A DESCRIPTION AND LIST OF THE LIGHTHOUSES OF THE WORLD. LONDON: RICHARD HOLMES LAURIE, 1866.

FRASER, ELLA. "A CHILDHOOD SPENT ON ISLE HAUTE," THE NOVA SCOTIAN, THE CHRONICLE-HERALD, 28 JANUARY 1989.

JOHNSTON, JOHN. "CANADA'S FIRST LIGHTHOUSE," THE ATLANTIC ADVOCATE, FEBRUARY 1986.

LANGTON-JONES, COMMANDER R. SILENT SENTINELS. LONDON: FREDERICK MULLER, 1944.

MACDONALD, SAMUEL COLLINS. "KEEPERS OF THE LIGHTS," WEEKLY CAPE BRETONER, 7 MARCH 1959.

MACKAY, DONALD. ANTICOSTI, THE UNTAMED ISLAND. TORONTO: MCGRAW-HILL RYERSON LIMITED, 1979.

MACKAY, MARY. "KEEPERS OF THE LIGHT DISAPPEARING FROM P.E.I," THE KINGS COUNTY WEEKLY, 18 JULY 1990.

MASON, LINDA. "SOUTH SHORE LIGHTHOUSE KEEPER RETIRES," THE CHRONICLE-HERALD, 7 SEPTEMBER 1991.

PHEMEISTER, MARTHA AND DORDON FULTON. SQUARE TAPERED WOODEN LIGHTHOUSES. OTTAWA: FEDERAL HERITAGE BUILDINGS REVIEW OFFICE, ARCHITECTURAL HISTORY BRANCH, 1990.

PLASKIN, MARY. "KEEPERS FADE BUT LIGHTS UNDIMMED," TRANSPO 82, WINTER.

PORTEOUS, SANDRA. "THE VANISHING BREED," THE DAILY NEWS SUNDAY MAGAZINE, 28 OCTOBER 1990.

PULLEN, REAR ADMIRAL HUGH F. "THE SEA ROAD TO HALIFAX," OCCASSIONAL PAPER NO. 1. HALIFAX: MARTIME MUSEUM OF THE ATLANTIC, 1980.

RICHARDSON, EVELYN M. WE KEEP A LIGHT. TORONTO: MCGRAW HILL-RYERSON, 1945.

RIGBY, CARLE A. ST. PAUL ISLAND, GRAVEYARD OF THE GULF, THE STORY OF A LITTLE KNOWN NOVA SCOTIAN ISLAND. HARTLAND: HARTLAND PUBLISHERS LTD., 1979.

SHAW, BARBARA. "THERE'S NO LIFE LIKE IT: REMINISCENCES OF LIGHTKEEPING ON SAMBRO ISLAND," THE NOVA SCOTIA HISTORICAL REVIEW, VOL. 3, NO. 1, 1983.

SLOCUM, JOSHUA. SAILING ALONE AROUND THE WORLD AND THE VOYAGE OF THE LIBERDADE. NEW YORK: COLLIER BOOKS, 1978.

STEPHENS, DAVID. LIGHTHOUSES OF NOVA SCOTIA. WINDSOR, NOVA SCOTIA: LANCELOT PRESS, 1973.

TAIT, THOMAS R. EARLY HISTORY OF LIGHTHOUSES, LIGHTHOUSE HISTORY AND STATUTES. EDINBURGH: JAMES HEDDERWICK, 1902.

TALBOT, FREDERICK. A. LIGHTSHIPS AND LIGHTHOUSES. LONDON: WILLIAM HEINEMANN, 1913.

THURSTON, HARRY. "THE LAST LIGHTHOUSE KEEPER," CANADIAN GEOGRAPHIC, MARCH/APRIL 1992.

TOWNSHEND, ADELE. "THE WRECK OF THE PHOENIX," THE ISLAND MAGAZINE, FALL/WINTER 1986.

WADE, WYN CRAIG. THE TITANIC, END OF A DREAM. NEW YORK: PENQUIN BOOKS, 1979.

WHITNEY, DUDLEY. THE LIGHTHOUSE. TORONTO: MCCLELLAND AND STEWART, 1975.

WICKENS, SONIA. SEAL ISLAND — AN ECHO FROM THE PAST. YARMOUTH: SONIA WICKENS, 1988.